Fun in the City

The Sound of Soft C

By Cynthia Amoroso

It is fun to
visit the city.

The city is a busy place.

A circus is in the city!

We walk on cement sidewalks in the city.

9

There are fun celebrations in the city.

We buy apple cider in the city.

13

14

We drive
in a circle
in the city.

We ride bicycles in the city.

18

In the center of the city is a fountain.

Now it is time to go to the cinema. This is a great city!

Word List:

bicycles

celebrations

cement

center

cider

cinema

circle

circus

city

place

Note to Parents and Educators

The books in this series are based on current research, which supports the idea that our brains are pattern-detectors rather than rules-appliers. This means children learn to read easier when they are taught the familiar spelling patterns found in English. As children encounter more complex words, they have greater success in figuring out these words by using the spelling patterns.

Throughout the series, the texts provide the reader with the opportunity to practice and apply knowledge of the sounds in natural language. The books introduce sounds using familiar onsets and *rimes*, or spelling patterns, for reinforcement.

For example, the word *cat* might be used to present the short "a" sound, with the letter *c* being the onset and "_at" being the rime. This approach provides practice and reinforcement of the short "a" sound, as there are many familiar words made with the "_at" rime.

The stories and accompanying photographs in this series are based on time-honored concepts in children's literature: well-written, engaging texts and colorful, high-quality photographs combine to produce books that children want to read again and again.

Dr. Peg Ballard
Minnesota State University, Mankato

Published by The Child's World®
1980 Lookout Drive • Mankato, MN 56003-1705
800-599-READ • www.childsworld.com

ACKNOWLEDGMENTS
The Child's World®: Mary Swensen, Publishing Director
The Design Lab: Design
Michael Miller: Editing

PHOTO CREDITS
© a katz/Shutterstock.com: 10; Akos Horvath/Shutterstock.
com: 6; Anelina/Shutterstock.com: 13; Christian Mueller/
Shutterstock.com: 18; Drop of Light/Shutterstock.com: 17;
holbox/Shutterstock.com: cover; Karramba Production/
Shutterstock.com: 21; Kateryna Tsygankova/Shutterstock.
com: 2; Linda Moon/Shutterstock.com: 5; nacroba/
Shutterstock.com: 14; vivanm/Shutterstock.com: 9

ISBN 9781503809307
LCCN 2015958472

Printed in the United States of America
Mankato, MN
June, 2016
PA02310

ABOUT THE AUTHOR

Cynthia Amoroso holds undergraduate degrees in English and elementary education, and graduate degrees in curriculum and instruction as well as educational administration. She is currently an assistant superintendent in a suburban metropolitan school district. Cynthia's past roles include teacher, assistant principal, district reading coordinator, director of curriculum and instruction, and curriculum consultant. She has extensive experience in reading, literacy, curriculum development, professional development, and continuous improvement processes.